GRRRROWL

HUNG

Neighborhood
friends...

Grrrrowlicious food for
hungry dogs

Jamie Young

Photography by Derek Swallwel

whitecap

ISBN 1-55285-868-5
ISBN 978-1-55285-868-4

Originally published by GRRRR™ Enterprises
PO Box 633, South Melbourne, Victoria, Australia 3205

Printed in Hong Kong by Midas Printing (Asia) Ltd.

While every attempt has been made to provide and apply the basic rules of nutrition the reader should not rely upon the work as a basis for professional or medical advice on the care and feeding of their dog. In any question of doubt concerning a dogs health or condition a pet healthcare professional's opinion should be sought. While Frodo likes every thing in this book, your dog might not.

a c k n o w l e d g e m e n t s

This book has been an amazing journey. Thank you to all the wonderful people who willingly gave their time, their kitchens, their shops, their clothes and yes, even their dogs! You all worked so hard to help make this a reality.

And to my best mate, chief taster and co-star, the reason for this book's being: Frodo. Where would the inspiration have come from without you?

Recipe development by Jamie Young
Photography by Derek Swalwell
Food styling & recipes by Georgia Young
Art direction by Angela Dressel
Design by Sarah Vincenzini
Written by Cate Lane
Edited by Nadine Boyd
Produced by Jamie Young

Thank you to Abby Fisher for additional recipes; Fitzroy Boulting at Equinox Management; Brett Murray at AG Clothing; Tony's Quality Meats at South Melbourne Market; Yurgen Plecko at The City Tiler; Driss Regague at Zelig Moroccan Interiors; Angela Riches; Simo and Stu; and Cherry's dads, Matt and Angelo.

In memory of Matilda.

Sources:
Jeni Edgley's Nutrition Book, Lansdowne Press, 1985; Give a Dog a Bone, Dr Ian Billinghurst; Raw Meaty Bones, Dr Tom Lonsdale; Doglopaedia, Ringpress Books, J.M. Evans and Kay White; www.ukrmb.co.uk.

contents

introduction

Food plays a big part in our lives. We love going to the market, inhaling the aromas, jostling for bargains and designing meals around seasonal produce. At home we fill the fridge with our fresh goodies and whip up our favorite recipe. Then, with our best friend salivating at our side, we open a can of processed offal and serve it to him. Puts you off that delicious meal you just ate, doesn't it?

Dogs originated from wolves and today still have the same digestive systems as their wild ancestors. Pet food companies continue to push the idea that dogs can happily thrive on processed food, but, as in life, it is always good to have an alternative.

And so started my endeavor to find out exactly what I needed to give my dog Frodo the best diet possible. The answers weren't easy to find. Some experts believe a cooked diet is the way to go, some think it should be raw and yet others say it should be mostly bones. But there wasn't one simple book that told me how I could feed him meals that are cheap, easy, balanced, nutritious and, most importantly, tasty.

With the help of some amazing friends (both two legged and four legged) I've produced a resourceful book that I hope will inspire you to make your own decision about your dog's diet and create some of the tastiest, healthiest meals your best friend has ever eaten.

I hope you and your dog enjoy making meals together!

Jamie Young

Apples
Fish fillets
Sardines
Pepper
Salt

10

c o o k e d

As I mentioned in the introduction, there are three schools of thought about what kind of diet your dog should have: cooked, raw and carnivore (bones & carcasses).

Dogs are like us – they like variety, things that taste good, and to be treated once in a while. Indulgent? I believe that by really mixing it up for Frodo – giving him a combination of all three not only nourishes his body but also his brain. Literally, it keeps him interested in life! This chapter covers a wide range of recipes for you to cook for your dog.

Author's note: I have used 'he', 'his' and 'him' throughout the book simply for the fact that I originally created these recipes for my boy, Frodo. Of course, this book is for all dogs, male and female.

puppy porridge

A nourishing meal for dogs who are young & young at heart!

1 cup rolled oats

2 cups puppy milk

1 teaspoon honey

1 tablespoon sultanas

1 tablespoon dried apple, chopped

Place all ingredients in a heavy-based saucepan and bring to the boil.

Continue to boil for one minute. Allow to cool before serving.

Makes one serving.

Cow's milk can cause allergies and bloating in many dogs. Puppy milk is available from pet stores.

This is Bobby

rice congee

Brown rice agrees with Frodo better than white. When it comes to rice, pasta and bread, try to serve brown whenever you can.

Otherwise known as The Killer of Flies

2 cloves garlic, finely chopped

1 chicken breast or thigh, skin on, chopped

1 carrot, finely chopped

1 celery stalk, finely chopped

1 cup brown rice

2 cups chicken stock (see page 26)

1 cup water

In a medium pot, sauté garlic with chicken, carrot and celery for 2–3 minutes.

Add rice and coat with pan juices.

Add liquid one cup at a time and keep mixture on a low simmer until rice is cooked.

More water can be added if necessary to cook rice through. Cool and serve.

Makes one serving.

fried rice

If your dog is anything like Frodo, watch out for the mess left on the floor!

This is Cherry

1 carrot

1 handful of green beans

1 handful of parsley

¼ cup peas, fresh or frozen

2 tablespoons olive oil

200g (7oz) minced lamb or veal

1 egg, lightly beaten

1½ cups cooked rice

Roughly chop vegetables or put them – peas excluded – in a food processor and process until fine.

Heat oil in a frypan and brown minced meat. Add the egg and lightly scramble. Add the vegetables and toss lightly to heat through. Add rice, increase heat and stir to separate the rice grains.

Pour the fried rice into a bowl, allow to cool before serving.

Makes one serving.

A little planning goes a long way. It'll save you money and also means you can buy in bulk.

fresh cooked sardines

The first time I cooked these, I couldn't stop picking at them – Frodo was lucky to get any!

1 tablespoon avocado oil

1 clove of garlic

4 freshly filleted sardines

1 cup broccoli, chopped

1 carrot, grated

1 ½ cups cooked rice

1 tablespoon yogurt

Heat oil in a frypan and sauté garlic gently. Add sardines and fry until cooked, being careful not to overcook.

Bring broccoli to the boil. Once slightly cooked, strain and allow to cool.

Mix remaining ingredients with broccoli and sardine mixture; serve.

Makes one serving.

Cherry can't seem to keep her tongue out of Frodo's mouth!

Veggies not being eaten?
Put them through a food processor
and mix them in with the meat.

15

f r i t t a t a

A tasty combination of meat, eggs and cheese - a true dog's delight!

1 tablespoon grapeseed oil

200g (7oz) minced chicken or pork

½ bunch spinach, chopped

2 medium potatoes, roughly chopped

4 eggs, lightly beaten

100g (3½ oz) cheddar cheese, grated

Heat oil in a heavy-based frypan and fry minced meat until cooked. Add spinach and allow to wilt. Pour into a bowl and set aside.

Boil potatoes until cooked. Strain and set aside. Slowly pour the eggs into frypan over medium heat. Add remaining ingredients and allow the frittata to puff and brown around the edges.

Finish cooking the frittata in a pre-heated oven or under the broiler for ten minutes.

Allow to cool before serving.

Makes one serving.

This is
Vulcan

Always allow food to come to room temperature before serving.

fish, vegetables & rice

Healthy and delicious! Frodo's coat always looks shinier after he eats fish.

1 tablespoon grapeseed oil

250g (10½ oz) oily fish

1 carrot, roughly chopped

1 cup leafy green vegetables, chopped

1 handful parsley, chopped

1 cup water

½ cup brown rice, cooked

In a medium sized pot heat oil and sear the fish. Add carrot, green vegetables, parsley and water.

Add rice, bring to a boil and turn heat down to simmer for five minutes.

Turn the heat off, cool and serve.

Makes one serving.

Convinced that pussy cats are there to be chased.

Choose green leafy vegetables such as Brussels sprouts, spinach, broccoli or swiss chard – they're full of vitamins!

pasta bolognese

This is great to make in a big batch and keep in the fridge or freezer.

This is Ricky

1 tablespoon olive or flaxseed oil

2 cloves garlic, chopped

500g (1¼ lb) beef or lamb mince

1 carrot, finely diced

1 celery stalk, finely chopped

2 large ripe tomatoes, roughly chopped

1 head broccoli, roughly chopped

250g (10½ oz) whole wheat pasta, cooked 'al dente'

In a medium sized pot, sauté garlic in oil. Add minced meat and fry until cooked.

Add carrot, celery, tomatoes and broccoli and cook through. Stir in pasta.

Allow to cool and serve with a few shaves of parmesan cheese mixed through.

Makes one serving.

To maintain nutrient levels (and taste), make sure you don't overcook food.

chicken meatballs

The first time I made these, Frodo rolled them around the floor before attacking them with delight!

Our happy little man

1kg (2¼ lb) minced chicken or pork

1 cup breadcrumbs

4 eggs, lightly beaten

100g (3½ oz) parmesan cheese

2 cloves garlic

1 handful of parsley, chopped

Pre-heat oven to 200°C (400°F).

Blend all ingredients in a food processor. Transfer mixture into a bowl.

Wet your hands to stop mixture from sticking and form into small balls.

Place in the oven on a tray lined with baking paper and cook for 15–20 minutes.

Serve just warm.

Makes 30–40 meatballs.

Make sure your dog has a big bowlful of fresh water with every meal.

rabbit stew

Rabbit is a huge favorite of Frodo's. It's cheap too!

This is Magnus

1 cup sweet potato, diced

1 tablespoon olive oil

250g (10½ oz) rabbit, diced

1 cup mushrooms, chopped

1 carrot, grated

1 handful of green beans, chopped

1 handful of parsley, chopped

Bring sweet potato to the boil then simmer gently until tender. Drain.

In a medium sized pan heat oil and fry rabbit until cooked.

Remove from heat and stir in mushrooms, carrot, beans, sweet potato and parsley.

Cool before serving.

Makes one serving.

You can also use minced rabbit in this dish – you'll find it at your pet store.

lamb, lentils & yogurt

Full of all the good things. Watch this get gobbled up!

1 tablespoon olive oil

200g (7oz) lamb, chopped

50g (2oz) chicken livers, diced

½ cup mushrooms, roughly chopped

3 medium sized tomatoes, chopped

100g (3½oz) lentils

1 cup of water

¼ cup fresh or frozen peas

1 tablespoon yogurt

In a medium sized pot or pan heat oil and fry lamb and livers until cooked through.

Add mushrooms, tomatoes and lentils; stir till combined, then add water and bring to the boil.

Turn down the heat and simmer till lentils are cooked, stirring occasionally.

When cooked, turn off the heat and add the peas. Cool, add yogurt and serve.

Makes one serving.

High fat meat may be appropriate for a dog with a big calorie requirement whereas a moderately active dog should have less.

Has a great love of digging.

21

steak, rice & vegetables

Trust me, the plate will be licked spotlessly clean!

This is Zoya

1 tablespoon olive oil

250g (10½ oz) of chuck steak, chopped

1 clove garlic, chopped

1 cup cooked rice

1 cup cabbage, chopped

1 carrot, grated

1 tablespoon cottage cheese

In a frypan heat oil and cook steak until just seared.

Add garlic and fry for one minute. Add rice and vegetables and stir until combined. Heat through for a few minutes.

Pour into a bowl and allow to cool.

Stir through cottage cheese and serve.

Makes one serving.

Once refrigerated food has come to room temperature stir in some oil, yogurt or cottage cheese to refresh the flavor.

pork, apple & oats

An interesting combination of textures: cooked and raw; chewy and crunchy.

1 tablespoon olive oil

250g (10½ oz) pork, diced

1 medium sweet potato, cooked and mashed

100g (3½ oz) greens (beans or spinach), roughly chopped

1 celery stalk, chopped

1 apple, chopped and deseeded

1 handful rolled oats

In a medium sized pot, heat oil and fry pork.

When cooked, add sweet potato, beans and celery and stir through.

Allow to cool, adding apple and rolled oats before serving.

Makes one serving.

Lower grade meat is not only cheaper, it's also better for your dog. Meat should only cost a few dollars per meal.

Loves to chase ducks after a protein shake!

ox tongue parcels

Tasty little packages just waiting to be crunched open.

This is Toffee

500g (1 ¼ lb) ox tongue, cubed

1 tablespoon olive oil

1 large carrot, chopped

¾ cup of peas

1 celery stalk, chopped

2 cloves garlic, finely chopped

1 handful of parsley, roughly chopped

1 bay leaf

500ml (1 pint) beef stock

2 sheets puff pastry

Pre-heat oven to 220°C (440°F).

Toss ox tongue in a little cornflour. Sauté in oil until well colored. On medium heat, add vegetables, garlic and bay leaf and stir. Fry until garlic begins to color, then add stock. Bring to a boil, turn the heat to low and cover. Cook for about 1 hour.

Remove the lid and reduce sauce until thick. Allow the mixture to cool, remove bay leaf.

Lay pastry sheets on the work surface and place equal portions of the mixture into the middle of each one.

To make each parcel, grab two corners of the sheet, roll over the mixture and press together at opposite corners. Cut away excess pastry.

Place in oven and bake for about 12 – 15 minutes or until golden brown.

Makes 2 parcels.

liver & vegetables

Packed with all the good stuff Frodo finds irresistible.

1 cup potatoes, chopped

1 cup pumpkin, chopped

1 tablespoon grapeseed oil

200g (7oz) of liver, kidneys, brains or heart, chopped

1 carrot, chopped

1 celery stalk, chopped

1 handful parsley, roughly chopped

Bring potatoes to a boil and simmer gently for a few minutes, then add pumpkin and cook until tender. Drain.

In a medium sized pan, heat oil and fry meat until cooked.

Add carrot, celery, pumpkin, potato and parsley and stir through. Allow to cool before serving.

Makes one serving.

When trying out something new, always check to see what comes out the other end to see how well your dog has processed the food.

Alias:
Ball Thief.

chicken or meat stock

A supply of home made stock is handy for adding flavour. Freeze some in an ice cube tray and use a cube at a time.

Making meals in batches makes sense. It means you won't be cooking all the time and you can simply take a meal out of the fridge or freezer and serve it quickly!

500g (1¼lb) chicken or lamb bones

½ onion, roughly chopped

1 carrot, roughly chopped

½ bunch parsley, chopped (stalks are fine)

1 celery stalk, roughly chopped

2 cloves garlic (optional)

Place bones in a large pot and cover generously with cold water. Bring to a simmer and skim off fat as it rises to the surface.

Add remaining ingredients.

Cook for 2 hours at a gentle simmer. Cool slightly then strain well. Refrigerate in a plastic container.

The next day skim off the solidified fat and pour the stock into ice cube trays or small containers.

Keep one container handy in the fridge and store the rest in the freezer.

Ruff buries his bones...
in daddy's bed!

r   a   w

Giving your dog a diet of raw meat and poultry, along with plenty of fresh fruit and vegetables provides him a classic raw food diet. It gives him all the essential nutrients he needs to keep him full of life, whilst giving you control over what he eats.

These easy to prepare recipes require no cooking and are great for when you have little time (who has these days?) and a hungry dog pestering you for food. Most will only take you a few minutes, making them the ultimate fast yet healthy food!

When I get home from the market, Frodo is beside himself with delight with all that meat in my basket! So I try to give him a raw meal or two when the food is really fresh – that way I know he's getting the best flavours and goodness.

And you can rest assured that serving food raw is unlikely to have any adverse effect on your dog.

f r e s h   m e a t y   b o n e s

I usually give Frodo his bone every morning after his walk. Lamb shanks head the list of his favorites.

1 shoulder or leg bone

There is nothing that will make a dog happier than a raw, meaty bone.

Make sure you vary the type of bone you feed your dog as different shaped bones clean different teeth.

And they also help reduce that dreaded dog breath!

(More about bones in the Carnivore chapter)

Only feed your dog raw chicken bones. Cooked ones may splinter.

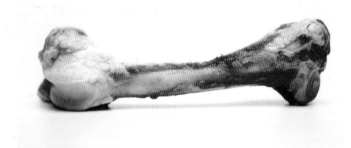

*This is
Biggles*

supper sardines

Frodo loves this because the oil from the can spreads through the rice
and the bread, adding heaps of flavour.

1 can sardines, (double layer in oil)

2 slices wholemeal bread, chopped

1 cup cauliflower, chopped

1 carrot, grated

1 cup cooked rice

1 tablespoon cottage cheese

Mix all ingredients together and serve.

Portion size depends not so much on the
size of your dog but how active he is. If
your dog is full of beans, make sure you
replace what he burns off.

*He knows how to
open the fridge.*

tasty health burgers

The perfect 'fast' food, packed with vitamins and ready to serve.

1kg (2¼lb) ground chicken

200g (7oz) ground beef

2 cloves garlic, roughly chopped

2 eggs

200g (7oz) ricotta cheese

200g (7oz) any green leaf vegetables

1 carrot, roughly chopped

1 tablespoon kelp powder

2 fish oil capsules

1 tablespoon flaxseed oil

Sesame seeds (optional)

Blend all ingredients in a food processor. Form into tennis ball-size portions, flatten into burgers and individually wrap and freeze. Defrost and serve as required.

Makes approximately ten.

Try using a variety of cuts of meat as the nutrient levels differ. Organ meat, for example, is very rich in nutrients whereas muscle meat is less so.

This is Scooter

mincemeat & greens

Change the meat and vegetables to give him as much variety as possible.

250g (10½ oz) ground meat
(lamb, veal, chicken, pork)

1 cup broccoli, chopped

2 brussels sprouts, finely chopped

½ cup peas

1 carrot, grated

1 tablespoon cottage cheese

1 tablespoon avocado oil

Mix all ingredients together and serve.

Make a batch of the vegetable mix and store in the fridge in a sealed plastic container for a few days, so you're not constantly chopping up vegetables.

Our little sleepy head

33

risotto stuffed chicken

Fine fare indeed. I serve this to Frodo on special occasions, like his birthday (or mine)!

Whenever you're making risotto for yourself, always make an extra portion to use in this recipe. Just make sure it has plenty of vegetables in it.

400ml (²/₃ pint) chicken stock (see page 26)

1 tablespoon olive oil

1 carrot, diced

1 celery stalk, diced

1 small bay leaf

1 pinch saffron (optional)

1 clove garlic, chopped

100g (3½ oz) Arborio rice

2 tablespoons parmesan cheese

1 handful of fresh herbs such as basil, parsley or mint, roughly chopped

Sea salt

1 small chicken

In a medium pot, bring the stock to a simmer. Keep on a low heat whilst cooking the risotto.

In a heavy-based pan, heat oil and sauté the carrot and celery for a few minutes then add the bay leaf, saffron and garlic. Sauté on a medium heat for 2 minutes or until the garlic starts to color.

Add rice to the mixture, coating it well and cook for another 2–3 minutes.

Slowly add the chicken stock, one cup at a time, allowing it to absorb before the next one is added, stirring constantly. Keep adding stock until the rice is tender. Remove bay leaf, add parmesan, herbs and salt, and mix through.

Allow the risotto to cool then spoon the mixture into the *raw* chicken. Place the bird in your dog's bowl and run!

steak or fish tartare

A true gourmet experience - great if you want to spoil your dog a little.

450g (1lb) ground beef or white fish fillets, finely chopped

2 egg whites

1 teaspoon flaxseed oil

1 small handful fresh chives, finely chopped

1 small handful parsley

½ teaspoon sea salt

Mix all ingredients together and process in a food processor.

For a more appealing texture push the mixture through a meat mincer and serve at once.

Daisy bites her nails.

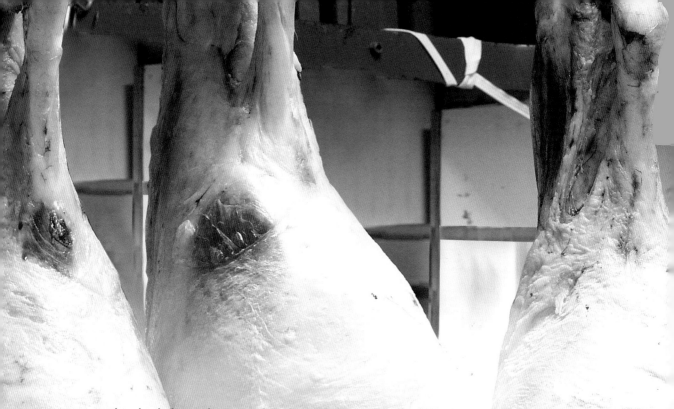

The third diet I discovered makes up around half of Frodo's meals. Essentially this diet replicates that of dogs in the wild. Meat and poultry carcasses top the menu, plus plenty of meaty bones. It's less about fruit and vegetables and more about fresh animal carcasses and offal. Sound good? Your dog will think so!

You can also use table scraps in small proportions. This is to satisfy the amount of omnivore food your dog would once have obtained by eating the intestines of his prey. If you're anything like me though, and don't have much left on your plate, then one or two meals from the cooked section will do the trick!

carnivore

c a r c a s s e s

These are cheap! You can pick them up at your local market or chicken shop.

During summer time, feed your dog with this type of food at night. That way there'll be fewer pesky flies!

Choose whole, fresh, cleaned carcasses from these animals:
> chicken
> turkey
> rabbit
> fish (large bones removed)

Large animal carcasses should be sawn into manageable pieces. Choose:
> goat
> lamb
> calf
> deer

Avoid bones that are too large or sawn lengthwise as your dog could chip a tooth. Also avoid too much fat on the bone.

Animal by-products that can also be used are pig's trotters, pig's and sheep's heads, brisket and rib bones.

As for quantity, an average dog should eat about 15 – 20% of their body weight a week.

o f f a l

Just like carcasses, offal is easy to obtain and extremely cheap
(much cheaper than canned dog food).

Choose fresh offal such as:
>liver
>lungs
>heart
>stomach
>digestive tracts
>tripe

Liver can be served once a week, whereas other offal should not exceed 50% of your dog's diet. Organ meat is not recommended for Dalmations.

If you run out of dog food, don't go reaching for the can – fast your dog just like in the wild.

Magnus is a gentle giant with a fetish for ABBA.

t r e a t s

Dogs love receiving treats and we love giving them, but don't overdo it! Use the treat as a reward for good behaviour. Have your dog 'do' something (no tricks, please!) to earn his treat.

Frodo gets his when he's helped me in the garden or he's brought back every ball that I've thrown to him. I usually let him eat the morsel out of my hand because it feels a bit more special that way. Remember to keep treats small, breaking them up into bite size pieces if necessary. Your dog will love them just the same!

doggy biscuits

Hope your pooch likes these as much as Frodo!

2 ¼ cups whole wheat flour

½ cup powdered milk

1 teaspoon salt

1 tablespoon brown sugar

1 cup sultanas

6 tablespoons butter or margarine

1 egg, lightly beaten

¼ cup iced water

Pre-heat oven to 180°C (360°F).

Mix flour, milk powder, salt, sultanas and sugar together. Add butter until mixture looks like cornmeal. Add egg then iced water. Form into a ball. Use more flour if required.

Pat out to 2cm (¾") thickness. Use doggie biscuit cutter to cut out shapes, or make your own shapes. Place on a baking tray and bake 25 – 30 minutes. Serve when completely cool.

Makes about 25 biscuits.

This is Tiger

cheese & bacon cookies

A tasty combination of meat, eggs and cheese – a true dog's delight!

Has two speeds: On and off.

¾ cup flour

½ teaspoon baking soda

½ teaspoon salt

⅔ cup butter

⅔ cup brown sugar

1 egg

1 teaspoon vanilla extract

1½ cups oats

1 cup cheddar cheese, shredded

½ cup wheatgerm

250g (10½ oz) bacon, trimmed of fat, chopped

Pre-heat the oven to 180°C (360°F).

Grease or line a baking tray. Combine flour, soda and salt in a medium bowl. Mix well and set aside.

In a large bowl, cream butter and sugar, then slowly beat in egg and vanilla. Add flour mixture, mixing thoroughly. Stir in oats, cheese, wheatgerm and bacon.

Drop spoonfuls of mixture onto a baking tray. Bake for 15–20 minutes or until brown.

Cool on a wire rack and serve, one or two at a time.

When completely cool, keep in an airtight container, in the fridge, for up to two weeks.

Makes about 15 cookies.

mock choc doughnuts

Try hiding these! I have to send Frodo outside when they are cooking!

*This is
Ruby*

*1⅓ cups whole wheat self rising flour **or**
1⅓ cups whole wheat flour and 2¼ tsp
baking powder*

1 egg, lightly beaten

½ cup beef or chicken stock

3 tablespoons peanut butter

250g (10½ oz) carob, chopped

Pre-heat oven to 200°C (400°F) and grease a baking tray. Place flour into a bowl, add in egg and stock, mixing well. Add peanut butter and form into dough. Roll dough into a ball.

On a lightly floured surface, roll out until it's approximately 2cm thick. Cut out pastry with small doughnut cutters. Re-roll scraps and repeat. Shape last bits by hand. Arrange doughnuts on tray and bake for 20 minutes until brown.

Allow to cool completely. Melt carob in a bowl in the microwave on low, checking and stirring every 30 seconds until melted. Using a teaspoon drizzle over the doughnuts and allow to cool on a wire rack.

Makes about 15 doughnuts.

Store in an airtight container when your dog isn't looking.

Ruby has been known to take off...
but then come home in a taxi.

This section is about different vitamins and minerals, their effects on your dog and where you can get a natural source of them without having to reach for the supplements.

Vitamins and minerals are essential to keep your dog in good health, and a deficiency in one can impair the function of the other. Quite simply, the key to a good diet is variety, and plenty of it!

vitamins

Vitamin A

Promotes bone growth and development, aids vision and skin maintenance. Vitamin A also maintains your dog's night vision. Find it in foods such as eggs, fish, carrots, leafy green vegetables, pumpkin, mangoes, apricots, peaches, sweet potatoes, cantaloupes, bananas, tomatoes, avocados, kelp, and fish oils. A deficiency of Vitamin A can retard growth, cause bone and skin disorders and vision problems.

B-complex

The B-complex vitamins help the body break down food for energy and help maintain the nervous system. This group of vitamins can be found in liver, dairy products, meats and whole grains. A deficiency of these nutrients can lead to health problems such as anaemia, constipation, drowsiness, eye and heart problems, indigestion, loss of appetite, nervousness, muscle weakness, paralysis, skin disorders and weight loss.

Vitamin B1

Boosts energy, gives support to all branches of the central nervous system. Found in almonds and other raw nuts, beans, red peppers, tongue and organ meats.

Vitamin B2

Assists in metabolism and the maintenance of hair, skin, nails and vision. Found in nuts, grains, liver, tongue, mushrooms and red capsicum.

Vitamin B3

Assists in energy production, improves circulation and reduces cholesterol and fat levels in the blood. Found in raw fish, lean meats, poultry, raw nuts, rolled oats and linseed.

Vitamin B5

Promotes healthy skin and nerves whilst aiding and bolstering other B group vitamins. Found in organ meats and whole grains.

Vitamin B6

Essential for the breakdown of carbohydrates, fats and proteins as well as the production of red blood cells and antibodies. Assists in absorption of Vitamin B12 and the normal functioning of the nervous, muscular and skeletal systems. Found in raw nuts and some fruits.

Vitamin B12

Essential for metabolizing amino acids and red blood cell formation. Found in brains, kidneys, muscle meats, fish, yogurt and cheese.

Vitamin C

Helps your dog fight infections. Found in most fresh fruit (particularly berries) all green vegetables, mushrooms and raisins.

Vitamin D

Promotes healthy bones and teeth whilst assisting in the absorption of calcium and phosphorus. Vitamin D deficiency can cause bone disorders and dental problems. Found naturally in egg yolks, cod liver oil and fish oils.

Sunlight also promotes the manufacture of Vitamin D. Taking your dog for a walk every day will ensure that he gets his share of the sun – although don't take him when it's too hot. Morning walks are usually best.

Vitamin D3

Promotes the growth of teeth and bones, and also regulates calcium & phosphorous absorption.

Vitamin E

Vitamin E aids reproduction and cell protection. It's essential for muscle function and is known for its ability to keep body cells from degenerating. Found in cereal grains, brown rice, avocado, spinach, Brussels sprouts, peas, celery, egg yolks and milk.

Vitamin K

Produced naturally in your dog's intestines. Vitamin K is important for the clotting of blood and also helps fight bacterial illness. Foods that contain Vitamin K include fish, raw green vegetables, yogurt, milk, egg yolks, fish liver oils and soybean.

Vitamin K3

Required for blood clotting (found in the same sources as Vitamin K).

Biotin

Essential for cellular growth of all tissue types and assists in energy levels. Found in raw nuts, cauliflower, salmon and tuna.

Calcium

Essential for the formation of bones and teeth, blood clotting, and nerve and muscle function. Found in almonds, soybeans, kelp, parsley, spinach, broccoli, celery and yogurt.

Choline

Essential for nerve and liver function and also aids fat metabolism. Choline is necessary to prevent severe liver disorders. Found in soybeans, egg yolks, spinach and liver.

Cobalt

Aids in vitamin B12 production. Can be found in liver, kidneys and milk.

Copper

Assists in the formation of blood haemoglobin and the formation of Vitamin C. Aids the digestive system, tissue respiration and healing process.

Folic Acid

Metabolizes amino acids, aids red blood cell formation and also aids vitamins B2 and C to form body protein and red blood cells. The intake of folic acid also has been found to improve your dog's appetite. Found in green leafy vegetables, fresh fruits, corn, mushrooms and avocado.

Iodine

Essential for the health of your dog's thyroid gland and all endocrine functions. Found in seafood and kelp.

Iron

Builds haemoglobin which transports oxygen throughout the body. Found in liver, whole grains, egg yolks, green leafy vegetables, sweet potatoes, garlic, soybeans, apricots, apples and avocadoes.

Magnesium

For strong bones and teeth, steady nerves and brain activity, lung tissue, blood fluidity, healthy glands and flexible joints. Found in lettuce, garlic, tomatoes, potatoes, bananas, raisins, almonds, kelp, cashews, soybeans, most whole grains, spinach, parsley, peas, brussels sprouts and celery.

Manganese

Helps to nourish the nerves and brain function, improves the digestion of fatty acids and cholesterol. Also assists in bone formation. Found in nuts, whole grains, green vegetables and egg yolks.

Niacin

Helps your dog to keep illnesses such as anaemia, dehydration, diarrhea, intestinal inflammation, nervous system disorders and mouth ulcers at bay. A natural ingredient in eggs, fish, meat and whole grains.

Pantothenic Acid

Conversion of carbohydrates to energy. A lack of pantothenic acid can lead to diarrhoea, poor appetite and a low resistance to disease. Found in soybeans and liver.

Phosphorus

Essential for feeding bones, teeth, hair and nails. Found in eggs, animal proteins and nuts.

Potassium

Sodium 'pulls' fluid in and potassium 'pushes' waste out. Supports, repairs and strengthens your dog's muscular system. Found in parsley, spinach, beetroot, avocado, kelp, raisins, whole grains, garlic and dried pears.

Sodium

Sodium is a fluid regulator that helps maintain nerve and muscle function. Found in celery, kelp, spinach, green vegetables, carrots, parsley, parsnip, garlic, cucumber, raisins, dried apricots, lentils and some fish.

Zinc

Essential for growth, healthy skin and tissue repair. Found in eggs and legumes.

In this section I've listed the oils I believe will have the most positive effects on your dog. Oils help nourish him inside and out – watch that coat shine! I simply mix a tablespoon of oil into every meal to keep Frodo happy and healthy! Alternate the ones you use as we've done in many of the recipes.

Cod liver oil	Rich in Vitamin A, D and the Omega-3 class fatty acids and important for protecting your dog against infections.
Wheat germ oil	An excellent source of Vitamin E complex.
Safflower oil	Great for cooking!
Olive oil	Extra-virgin olive oil is the most digestible of the edible fats. It helps to assimilate Vitamins A, D and K; contains essential acids, slows the aging process, whilst helping bile, liver and intestinal functions. Great for cooking.
Flaxseed oil	Flaxseed delivers the full benefits of omega 3, 6 & 9 essential fatty acids, plus all of the fibre, protein, vitamins, minerals and amino acids that are important for overall good health.
Avocado oil	Research has shown that avocado is full of mono-unsaturated fats, which are the 'good' fats that help reduce the 'bad' cholesterol in the bloodstream.
Grapeseed oil	Grapeseed extract is sourced from the seeds of red grapes, and is a flavonoid with extremely potent anti-oxidant properties. Anti-oxidants help scavenge free radicals that are known to damage cell DNA. It's also believed that grapeseed has cancer fighting properties.

o i l s

animal

Through trial and error, I've devised a list of Frodo's favorites to help you create your own recipes. There may be some foods that your dog simply doesn't like but you should find plenty of equally good alternatives here.

In the raw   Meaty bones from lamb, beef, rabbit, chicken and pork.
              Muscle meat from chicken, lamb, beef and pork.
              Organ meat such as liver, kidneys, brain, heart and intestines.*

Get clucky   Eggs, especially the yolk.

Say cheese!   Plain cheeses such as cheddar, Swiss and parmesan,
              cottage cheese, yogurt and goat's milk.

Gone fishin' Oily fish fillets such as herring, salmon and sardines.
              Always wash thoroughly and remove large bones, head, fins and gizzards.

              *Organ meat is not recommended for Dalmatians.

vegetable

While your dog would probably be happy if you served him meat, meat and more meat, it's important that he has plenty of veggies, cereals and fruit to keep him happy and healthy. Like kids, dogs sometimes need to be trained to eat their vegetables and I find that if Frodo sees me eating a carrot, he'll want some too!

Green and leafy	Serve as much of these vegetables as your dog will eat: spinach, broccoli, outer leaves of lettuce (washed), cauliflower, broccoli and Brussels sprouts.
Other vegetables	Asparagus, beans (string), beetroot, carrot, cabbage, celery, capsicum (seeds removed), corn (tinned or fresh, removed from the cob), mushrooms, parsnip, peas (fresh or frozen) potatoes (cooked), pumpkin (cooked), squash, tomatoes and turnip.
Fruit	Fresh and dried fruits such as apples, avocados, bananas, blueberries, grapes, melons, pears, peaches, plums and raisins. Serve plenty of fresh fruit and less dried (it can be quite high in sugar) by cutting it into small pieces and adding it to the meal you're preparing. Or serve it as a treat.
Cereals and grains	Whole-grains, brown rice and rolled oats, wheatgerm, wheatbran and wheatmeal bread. Try to avoid white cereals and grains such as white rice, bread and pasta, as they often cause bloating and wind.
Herbs	Choose fresh herbs such as basil, dandelion greens, fennel, mint and parsley.

t o x i c

There are some things that you should never feed your dog. Some dogs may have allergies to particular foods – you'll find out quickly enough if there's something that doesn't agree with your dog. This is a general guide (not an exhaustive list) on the things that no dog should ever eat – there may be other things that you find out simply by trial and error.

Say no to...

Too much onion and garlic (small amounts are fine)

Chocolate. Some dogs may be able to have small amounts but it's best not to risk it

Mouldy cheeses and soft cheeses with rinds such as camembert and brie. These can cause allergic reactions, so it's best to stick to plain, firm textured cheeses

Raw potato

Apple seeds

Cherry or olive pits

i n d e x